FOREST ANIMALS

FOREST ANIMALS

JULIANNA PHOTOPOULOS

Published by Amber Books Ltd
United House
North Road
London
N7 9DP
United Kingdom

www.amberbooks.co.uk
Facebook: amberbooks
YouTube: amberbooksltd
Instagram: amberbooksltd
X(Twitter): @amberbooks

ISBN: 978-1-83886-365-4

Project Editor: Anna Brownbridge
Designer: Andrew Easton
Picture Research: Adam Gnych

Printed in China

Contents

Introduction

Almost one-third of our planet is covered by areas with a large number of trees – or forests. Found on every continent except Antarctica, forests provide food and shelter for many animals, plants, and people. They also give us oxygen, regulate the climate, purify water, and slow the rate of climate change. There are typically three types of forests: temperate, tropical and boreal. Temperate forests, with trees such as oaks and birch, are home to deer, squirrels, bears and wolves. These forests are found across eastern North America, Europe, Asia and parts of South America. The hot tropical forests – from rainforests to mangroves – are located in areas near the equator, such as Southeast Asia, sub-Saharan Africa and Central America. Chimpanzees, jaguars and anacondas live in tropical forests. Finally, reindeer and moose can be found among pine trees or conifers in the usually freezing boreal forests, or taiga, across Siberia, Scandinavia and North America. The world of forest animals will undoubtedly enchant, but we also need the hidden power of these animals to disperse seeds, pollinate and restore our forests.

ABOVE:
The critically endangered red wolf (*Canis rufus*) is only found in the wild in North Carolina, United States.

OPPOSITE:
A black howler (*Alouatta caraya*), or black-and-gold howler, sits on a tree branch in South America. Males are completely black while females and babies have gold coats.

Asia

Asia is the largest and most populous continent. The continent's tropical rainforests stretch across much of southern Asia while coniferous and deciduous forests lie farther north. Indian forests – home to about 90,000 animal species – include tropical evergreen and deciduous forests, swamps, mangroves, sub-tropical, montane, scrub and alpine forests.

Many native animals in Asia have adapted perfectly to their forest environments. For instance, the stripes of tigers and the skin colour and texture of mossy frogs help these animals stay hidden in their natural surroundings. Rainforest animals – from reptiles like the paradise flying snake to mammals like the Sunda flying lemur – have developed the ability to glide, or 'fly', through the air, quickly moving undetected from tree to tree. On the other hand, those animals that cannot fly or glide are usually quite small and light, which helps them travel to trees' most slender upper layers in the lush, warm, and wet forest.

However, the massive expansion of the continent's human population has put huge pressure on the animals that live in Asia. As a result, many species are endangered and face a number of threats, such as habitat loss, which risk wiping them off the face of the earth.

OPPOSITE:
Sumatran tiger
A close-up of the critically endangered Sumatran tiger or *Panthera tigris sumatrae* native to the Indonesian island of Sumatra. It is the smallest of all tigers, measuring up to 2.55m (8.4ft).

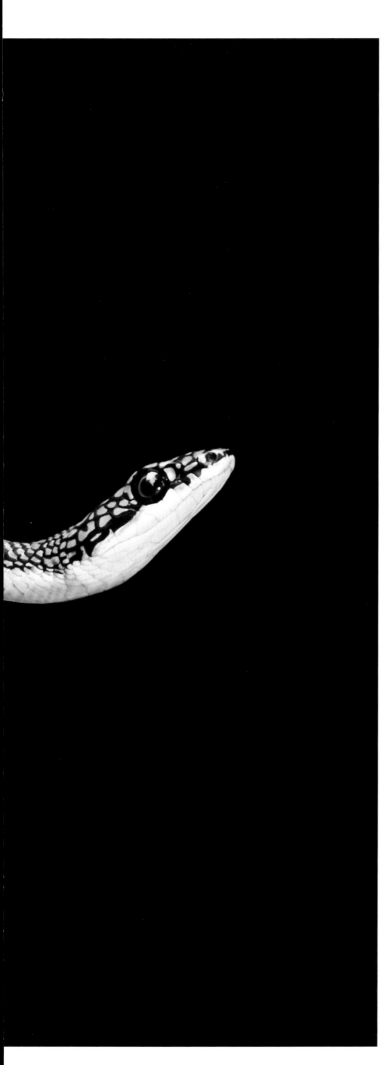

ALL PHOTOGRAPHS:
Paradise flying snake
This mildly venomous snake species, *Chrysopelea paradisi*, is found mostly in the moist forests of Southeast Asia. It can glide 10m (33ft) from treetops or rocks by stretching and flattening its body in mid-air. *C. paradisi* is a constrictor and can swallow its prey (e.g. lizards) whole.

Wallace's flying frog
Named after English naturalist
Alfred Russell Wallace, this
flying frog species (*Rhacophorus
nigropalmatus*) lives mostly in
trees and glides from tree to tree
with the help of its webbed feet.
Despite their large size – about
10cm (4in) in length – Wallace's
flying frogs cling to slender twigs
without hesitation.

RIGHT TOP:

Brown fish owl

The owl species *Ketupa zeylonensis*, with golden-yellow eyes and feathery ear tufts, is found from Turkey to South and Southeast Asia. Often spotted on rocks near water to hunt, it grabs mostly fish, frogs and crabs for dinner.

RIGHT BOTTOM:

Indian eagle-owl

Also known as the Bengal or rock eagle-owl, this large owl species (*Bubo bengalensis*) lives in scrub forests in the Indian subcontinent. *B. bengalensis* was previously considered a subspecies of the Eurasian eagle-owl (*B. buba*), but is smaller and has a black-bordered facial disk.

OPPOSITE:

Japanese badger

As the name suggests, this species of badger (*Meles anakuma*) is endemic to Japan. Japanese badgers are close relatives to European (*M. meles*), Asian (*M. leucurus*) and Caucasian (*M. canescens*) badgers but have less distinct facial stripes.

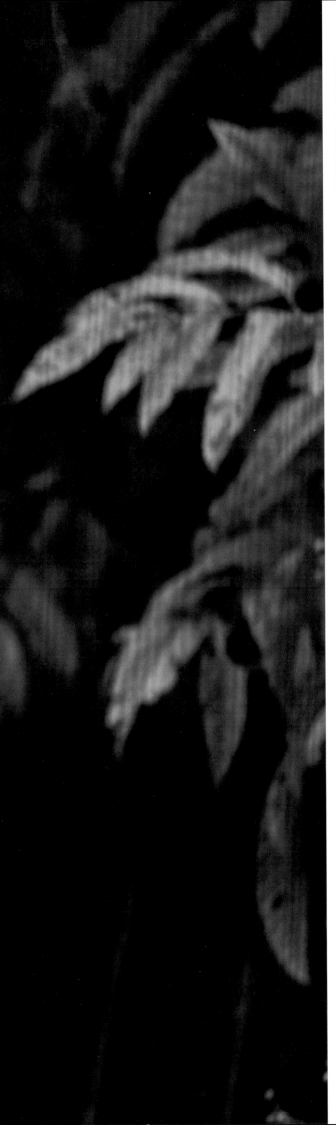

LEFT:

Orangutan

Members of the *Pongo* genus are commonly known as orangutans – the Malay word for 'man of the forest'. With distinctive red fur and long, strong arms to help them move through the Indonesian and Malaysian rainforests, orangutans are the largest tree-dwelling mammals. All three orangutan species are critically endangered.

ABOVE BOTH:

Strong bond

Orangutans are the most solitary of the great apes, but mothers and their young share a strong bond. Infants will stay with their mothers for up to eight years until they have learned how to survive on their own.

Bengal tiger
Among the biggest living wild cats, the charismatic Bengal tiger or *Panthera tigris tigris* is a native tiger subspecies of the Indian subcontinent. It is the most common tiger – though endangered – and makes up about half of all wild tigers. Thanks to its stripes, the tiger can blend into its forest habitat.

ABOVE:
Proboscis monkey
In the wild, proboscis monkeys
or long-nosed monkeys (*Nasalis
larvatus*) live in the jungles
of Borneo, often near coastal
mangroves. However, only males
live up to their name, with long-
protruding noses to attract
the females.

RIGHT:
Philippine tarsier
This curious-looking animal is one
of the world's smallest primates,
measuring between 8.5cm (3.4in)
and 16cm (6.3in). An endangered
species, the Philippine tarsier or
Carlito syrichta is being protected
in its native Philippines.

OPPOSITE:
Red panda
Normally found in the temperate
forests of the eastern Himalayas
and southwestern China, the
endangered red panda or *Ailurus
fulgens* has nearly disappeared in
the wild. At about 55.8–63.5cm
(22–25in) long, the red panda is
about the size of a large house cat.

LEFT:

Spot-bellied eagle-owl
This impressive-looking large pair of spot-bellied eagle owls, also known as the forest eagle-owl and *Ketupa nipalensis*, lives in the forests of the Indian subcontinent and Southeast Asia.

ABOVE:

Yellow-throated marten
The marten species *Martes flavigula* is native to Asia. It is the largest marten in the Old World, measuring 50-72cm (19.7-28.3in) without its long tail which makes up more than half its length.

25

RIGHT:
Sunda flying lemur
The species *Galeopterus variegatus* lives in the trees throughout the tropical rainforests of Southeast Asia. Here, a young Sunda flying lemur is peering from beneath its mother's body.

FAR RIGHT:
Gliding mammal
The Sunda flying lemur is a skillful climber but cannot truly fly. Instead it glides from tree to tree – over a distance of up to 100m (328ft) – thanks to a parachute-like membrane called *patagium*.

Kuhl's flying gecko
Named after the German zoologist Heinrich Kuhl, Kuhl's flying gecko (*Gekko kuhli*) is well-adapted to the forests of Southeast Asia. Except for its excellent camouflage, it has long flaps on both sides of its body, webbed feet and a flattened tail which allows it to glide over short distances.

Emerald ash borer

Agrilus planipennis, or the emerald ash borer, is a metallic wood-boring beetle species native to northeastern Asia. The females lay eggs in bark crevices of ash trees which larvae later feed on.

RIGHT BOTTOM:

Mango tree borer

This insect species (*Batocera rufomaculata*) belongs to the Cerambycidae family, also known as long-horned beetles. With over 35,000 species, most long-horned beetles have extremely long antennae which are often as long as or longer than their body.

OPPOSITE:

Leaf-mimic katydid

A master of camouflage, this leaf-like bush cricket, or katydid, is native to northern Borneo. While the males of the *Eulophophyllum lobulatum* species are green and blend into the forest leaves, the females stand out in red and pink.

Reticulated python
The species *Malayopython reticulatus*, or the reticulated python, can be found in South and Southeast Asia. It is the longest snake in the world, reaching over 6m (20ft) in length.

LEFT:

Northern white-cheeked gibbons

Nomascus leucogenys, commonly known as the Northern white-cheeked gibbon, forms small family groups usually consisting of two adults and a baby. Here, a beige-coloured female breastfeeds her baby while looking at the male, who has a black coat and white patches on his cheeks.

ABOVE TOP:

Siamang

The tree-dwelling black-furred gibbon Siamang or *Symphalangus syndactylus* lives in the forests of Indonesia, Malaysia and Thailand. Siamangs can be twice the size of other gibbons – at up to 1m (3.3ft) in height and 14kg (30.8lb) in weight – making them the largest gibbon.

ABOVE BOTTOM:

Great hornbill

The distinctive large, curved, bright yellow beak belongs to the great hornbill or *Buceros bicornis*. Great hornbills are the heaviest Asian hornbills, weighing between 2kg (4.4lb) and 4kg (8.8lb). Here, a male great hornbill – distinguished by its red eyes – flies in the forest with food in his beak.

Vietnamese mossy frog
This eye-catching frog species (*Theloderma corticale*) resembles a clump of moss, as its common name suggests. Found in Vietnam, Laos and China, the Vietnamese mossy frog curls into a ball and plays dead when frightened.

Sun bear

Named for its distinctive chest patch, the sun bear (*Helarctos malayanus*) spends most of its time in trees found in the tropical forests of Southeast Asia. Its up to 25-centimetre-long (9.8in) tongue can reach insects in tight spaces and honey from beehives. *H. malayanus* is the smallest bear species, measuring about 1-1.4m (3.3-4.6ft) long.

ALL PHOTOGRAPHS:

Binturong

Also known as a bearcat due to its appearance, the binturong (*Arctictis binturong*) lives in the tropical forests of South and Southeast Asia. It has an extremely long tail which helps it move on tree branches and grasp them. Binturongs smell like buttered popcorn from a substance they use to mark branches and foliage in their territories.

Africa

Almost one-fourth of Africa – the second-largest continent – is covered with forests. These forests range from the lush and wet lowland tropical rainforests to the drier woodlands in the highlands and savannahs. However, most of Africa's native rainforest has been destroyed by development, agriculture, and forestry.

Today, most of the continent's remaining rainforests are found across six countries in western and central Africa, along the Congo River basin. In fact, the Congo Basin contains one of the world's largest tropical rainforests – second only to the Amazon in South America, and crucial for regulating the world's climate. It is also home to over 2,000 animal species, including one of Africa's most aggressive, the safari ants, and some of the most endangered: gorillas, chimpanzees, bonobos, forest elephants, and the okapi.

Off the southeastern coast of Africa lies the island of Madagascar, known for its forests' unique plant and animal diversity. Five percent of the world's species live on this island – from the ring-tailed lemurs to gremlin-like ayes-ayes – most of which are native and found nowhere else in the world.

African animals are important pollinators of the continent's forests. But sadly, deforestation and poaching in the forests of Africa have caused many animal populations to decline, or even become extinct.

OPPOSITE:
Grey parrot
This highly social species, *Psittacus erithacus*, is known for its ability to mimic human speech. It is native to the rainforests of Central Africa.

Ring-tailed lemur
As the name suggests, this
endangered lemur has a long and
black-and-white ringed tail. Ring-
tailed lemurs (*Lemur catta*) are
highly social, living in groups of
up to 30 individuals on the island
of Madagascar, with the females
being in charge.

African forest buffalo
The subspecies *Syncerus caffer
nanus* is found in the rainforests
of Central and West Africa.
Also known as the dwarf or
Congo buffalo, it is the smallest
subspecies of African buffaloes,
weighing on average about
270kg (600lb).

Mountain gorilla
This endangered gorilla
subspecies, *Gorilla beringei
beringei*, lives in the forests of
southwestern Uganda and the
Virunga mountains in Central
Africa, though only about 1000
remain in the wild. Older adult
males are called silverbacks
because of the broad strip of
silver hair on their backs.

Chimpanzees

These endangered great apes (*Pan troglodytes*) live in groups of 15–150 individuals led by a male. Many populations are found in tropical rainforests but can also be seen in woodlands and grasslands across Central and West Africa. Chimpanzees are among our closest living relatives, sharing 98.7 per cent of our genetic blueprint.

ABOVE:
Bonobo
Once called the pygmy chimpanzee, the endangered bonobo (*Pan paniscus*) is native only to the forests on the left bank of the Congo River. Like their chimpanzee cousins, bonobos are the closest living relatives to humans.

RIGHT:
Ground pangolin
Smutsia temminckii is one of the four African species of pangolins and the only one found in eastern and southern Africa. Pangolins, like anteaters, have long snouts and even longer tongues, which they use to eat ants and termites.

OPPOSITE:
Aye-aye
This rare lemur species of Madagascar, *Daubentonia madagascariensis*, is the world's largest nocturnal primate. Aye-ayes have peculiar features, such as huge ears, rodent-like teeth, a bushy tail and a long middle finger to poke grubs out of trees.

LEFT:

Impala

The medium-sized antelope called impala or *Aepyceros melampus* is known for its long, spiral horns, which males use to challenge each other. The females, on the other hand, are hornless. Impalas are found in eastern and southern Africa.

ABOVE:

Fossa

This cat-like creature, *Cryptoprocta ferox*, is in fact a close relative of the mongoose. The fossa is the largest mammal predator of Madagascar and preys on anything it can get its claws on, including lemurs and rodents.

ALL PHOTOGRAPHS:

African bush elephant

Loxodonta africana, commonly known as the African bush or savanna elephant, is the world's largest living land animal. Adult males can weigh almost 11 tonnes (13,000lb) and reach 3.96m (13ft) tall at the shoulder. They generally travel alone or in groups of their own, while females and young travel in herds.

African forest elephant
This critically endangered elephant species, *Loxodonta cyclotis*, is smaller and rarer than its endangered cousin, the African bush elephant. Unlike its cousin, who thrives in different habitats, *L. cyclotis* only lives in tropical forests in West Africa and the Congo Basin. Here, one uses its trunk as a snorkel while wading in deep water.

Guttural toad
A male *Amietophrynus gutturalis* calls from the surface of water in southern Africa. Males call throughout the year but the guttural 'snores' are louder in October and November during the breeding period.

Giraffe weevil
Named for its giraffe-like neck, the giraffe weevil (*Trachelophorus giraffa*) is found on giraffe beetle trees, where it feeds on its leaves. Males use their necks, which are two to three times longer than females', to fight off other males.

Goliath beetle
Members of the *Goliathus* genus are among the largest insects in the world. This male of the species *Goliathus goliatus*, native to tropical Africa, measures between 6cm (2.36in) and 11cm (4.33in).

African leopard
The captivating big cat *Panthera pardus pardus* rests on a rock behind some bushes in Sub-Saharan Africa. African leopards are mainly active from dusk until dawn and will rest for most of the day in bushes, among rocks or on tree branches.

African civet
At first glance, the African civet or *Civettictis civetta* looks like a raccoon. However, it is larger, and its body has black and white markings. Native to Sub-Saharan Africa, African civets are known to secrete a musk that has been used in the perfume industry.

RIGHT BOTTOM:
Bongo
This forest-dwelling antelope, *Tragelaphus eurycerus*, can be recognized by its distinctive white stripes against a striking chestnut coat. It is native to Sub-Saharan Africa.

OPPOSITE:
Gabino viper
This long tongue, used to smell, belongs to the West African venomous viper *Bitis rhinoceros*, also known as the Gabino or West African Gaboon viper. Gabino vipers have two distinctive horns on their snout and one black triangle under each eye.

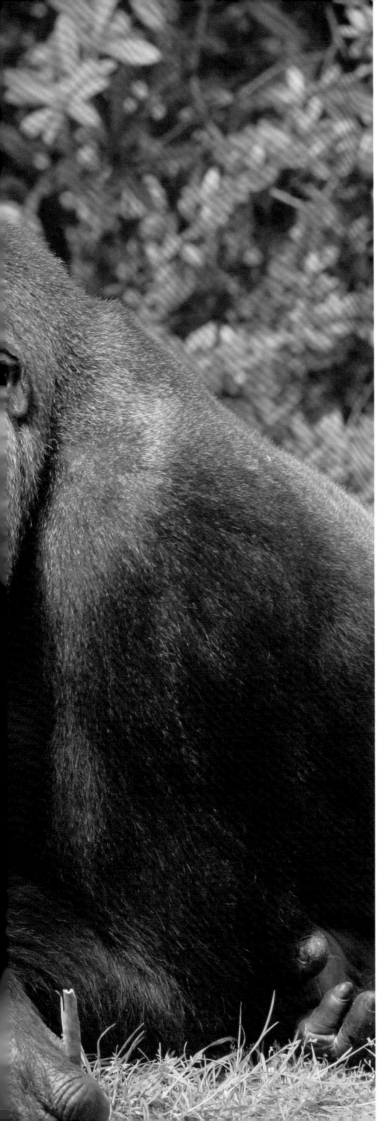

ALL PHOTOGRAPHS:

Western lowland gorilla
Found across Central and West
Africa, the subspecies *Gorilla
gorilla gorilla* is the most
widespread gorilla. However, it is
still critically endangered. Western
lowland gorillas are the smallest
subspecies of the *Gorilla* genus,
but a male can still reach 1.8m
(5.9ft) in height and weigh up
to 270kg (595lb).

Eastern lowland gorilla
Also known as Grauer's gorilla,
the eastern lowland gorilla
or *Gorilla beringei graueri* is
the largest subspecies of the
Gorilla genus. Males can weigh
up to 209kg (461lb) and stand
1.96m (6.43ft) tall. Eastern
lowland gorillas, endemic to the
mountainous forests of the east
of the Democratic Republic of the
Congo, are critically endangered.

LEFT:

Lowland streaked tenrec

This small, spiny, shrew-like creature is the lowland streaked tenrec (*Hemicentetes semispinosus*). It is found in the rainforests of Madagascar, often splashing in shallow waters or digging around.

ABOVE TOP:

Zebra duiker

Cephalophus zebra is an antelope with zebra-like stripes on its back. This allows it to blend into the forests of midwestern parts of Africa.

ABOVE BOTTOM:

Red river hog

Named for its red coat and fondness for wading in water, the red river hog or *Potamochoerus porcus* lives in West and Central Africa.

Arum lily frog

Named for often being found in arum lily flowers, the arum lily frog (*Hyperolius horstockii*) is native to South Africa. Arum lily frogs, also known as Horstock's arum-frogs or Horstock's reed frogs, can change colour to camouflage themselves but have to hide their bright orange feet under their bodies.

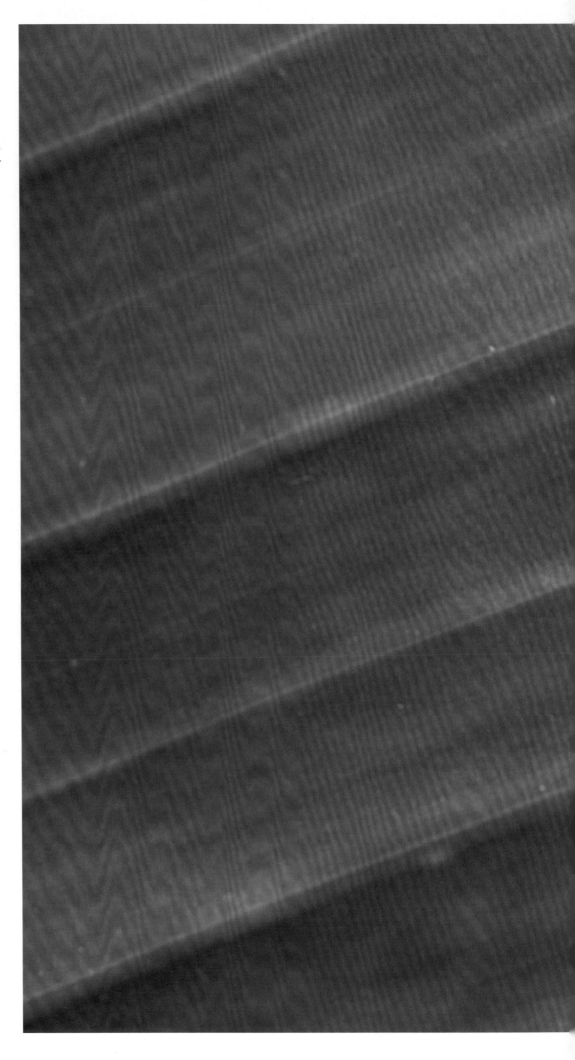

Safari ants
Members of the *Dorylus* genus are known as safari ants, driver ants, or siafu. These fierce ants have large heads with powerful scissor-like mandibles which they can use to snack on rats in central, eastern and southern Africa, and tropical Asia. At 4-6.3cm (1.6-2.5in) long, safari ant queens are the largest living ants in the world.

Grey foam-nest tree frog
Named for making foam nests, grey foam-nest tree frogs (*Chiromantis xerampelina*) are found in southern Africa. Like other tree frogs, *C. xerampelina* has discs on its toes to attach to surfaces, such as trees.

Nesting site
Female grey foam-nest tree frogs make foam nests above water by whipping up a sticky discharge with their back legs. Into this protective foam, they lay 500–1250 eggs, which are fertilized by multiple males. When tadpoles are four to six days old, they drop into the water below.

Adaptation
Grey foam-nest tree frogs can change colour – between dark brown and chalky white – to adapt to temperature changes. Out of the water on hot days, the frogs are able to reflect heat by turning white, secrete a wax-like substance to stop hydration and conserve water by concentrating urine.

Natal forest tree frog
This South African species,
Leptopelis natalensis, lives in the
leaves and branches of forest trees.
The species name *natalensis* means
'from Natal' – the former name of
KwaZulu-Natal, where this tree
frog is found.

African foam-nest tree frog
Chiromantis rufescens is found in
the tropical rainforests of Central
Africa. African foam-nest tree
frogs get their name from building
nests of foam that overhang the
water. These tree frogs mate in a
position called amplexus, where
the male clasps the female while
on her back.

Starry night reed frog
From Madagascar, the beautiful frog species *Heterixalus alboguttatus* sits on a leaf. The 11 members of the *Heterixalus* genus are commonly known as Madagascar reed frogs because they are endemic to Madagascar.

LEFT:

Okapi

This endangered forest species (*Okapia johnstoni*) looks like a cross between a deer and a zebra. However, the okapi, or forest giraffe, is closely related to the giraffe. While all males have horns, females have bumps or hair whorls. Okapis are native to the Ituri Rainforest in the Democratic Republic of Congo.

ABOVE TOP:

Tongue

Okapis use their long, dark tongues to pluck buds and leaves from branches, as well as to groom their ears and eyes. Their tongues are about 46cm (18in) long.

ABOVE BOTTOM:

Zebra-like stripes

The distinctive stripes of the okapi resemble those of a zebra. These stripes appear like streaks of sunlight coming through the trees, which help okapis blend into their forest environment.

Hairy bush viper
Named for its bristly hair-like look, the hairy bush viper (*Atheris hispida*) lives in the rainforests and bushes of Central Africa.

North America

The third-largest continent, North America, extends from the tiny Aleutian Islands in the northwest and the huge island of Greenland in the northeast to the Isthmus of Panama in the south.

In the northern territories, many animals have adapted to live in the cold, subarctic climate of the boreal forests, or taiga. The travelling caribou in their thick winter coats, for example, can dig through the snow with their large hooves in search of food. Whereas often more colourful animals in the tropical forests of Central America, such as sloths, monkeys, and birds, are used to a warmer climate and spend most of their time well-camouflaged in the lush, green trees and foliage. North American forests also host the iconic black and grizzly bears, bison, moose, and elks in the United States and Canada.

The sheer scope of the North American continent means that very distinct animals in various forest habitats – like the caribou and spider monkeys that are found on opposite corners of North America – still share the same continent. This leads to an incredibly beautiful and diverse spread of forest animal species in North America.

OPPOSITE:
Caribou
The large-hoofed caribou and reindeer are the same species – *Rangifer tarandus*. However, caribou are native to North America, whereas reindeer are native to northern Europe and Asia.

ABOVE:
Red-eyed tree frog
Native to forests from Central America to northwestern South America, the red-eyed tree frog gets its name from its distinctive bright red eyes. These eyes can scare predators away if the frog's green-coloured camouflage fails.

RIGHT:
Resplendent quetzal
This strikingly coloured bird lives in the mountainous, tropical forests of Central America. During mating season, the tail feathers of the males grow and form a spectacular green train. It is the national bird of Guatemala.

OPPOSITE:
Cougar
The magnificent *Puma concolor* species is the largest native American cat. Though large like a big cat, it belongs to the smaller cat subfamily called *Felinae*. *P. concolor* is commonly known by many names, such as cougar, puma and panther.

Elk
A herd of elk or *Cervus canadensis* at the National Elk Refuge in Jackson Hole, Wyoming. Elk are related to deer but are much larger than most of their relatives. Only male elks have antlers, which they lose each year in March.

Striped skunk
This adorable North American
baby animal is a striped skunk
or *Mephitis mephitis*. When
threatened, the skunks stand in
a defensive position ready to use
their stinky spray from up to about
3m (10ft) away – though kits, or
baby skunks, have a limited supply
of spray and so use it wisely!

Eastern chipmunk
Tamias striatus or the eastern
chipmunk is known to carry food
like seeds, fruits or nuts in its
cheek pouches. It climbs trees
in the eastern United States and
southern Canada and builds its
nests underground.

American badger
Though this badger, *Taxidea
taxus*, looks like the European
badger, they are not closely
related. However, both are
members of the **Mustelidae**
family, which has about 70 species,
including weasels, otters, martens,
ferrets and wolverines.

LEFT:

Moose

Alces alces, or the moose, is the largest species of deer, weighing as much as 820kg (1808lb). Moose have wide hooves, which help them walk in the snow or muddy grounds because they typically live in areas – in Canada, the USA, Europe and Russia – that have cold, snowy winters.

ABOVE:

Long legs

Moose have long legs that allow them to wade easily through deep water or snow. They can also run very fast – up to 56km/h (35mph) over shorter distances and 32km/h (20mph) over longer runs.

91

RIGHT TOP:

American marten

Martes americana is found in northern areas of North America, from Newfoundland and Nova Scotia to Alaska. It is well-adapted to snow with its thick fur and large furry paws, which allow it to keep warm and travel easily over deep snow.

RIGHT BOTTOM:

Buck

This white-tailed deer is a male – or buck – recognized by its antlers. Only males grow antlers which they shed and regrow every year. Antlers help males attract mates and fight other males or predators.

OPPOSITE:

White-tailed deer

Named for their tails' white underside, white-tailed deer (*Odocoileus virginianus*) are the smallest members of the *Cervidae* (deer) family in North America. White-tailed deer are native to places from southern Canada to South America.

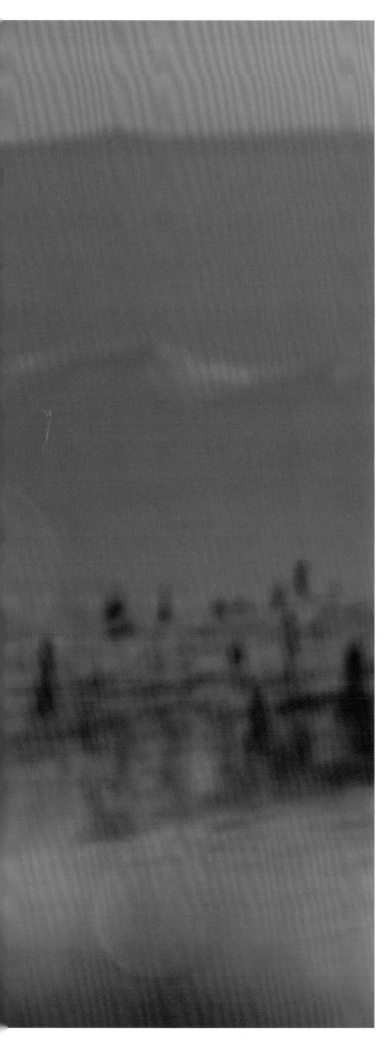

ALL PHOTOGRAPHS:

Caribou

This deer species, *Rangifer tarandus*, is the only in which both male and females have antlers, although this varies by subspecies. Only the males shed and grow back their antlers. Caribou have hollowed hooves, which allow them to dig through the snow when looking for food.

Mule deer
Nicknamed 'the deer of the west',
mule deer (*Odocoileus hemionus*)
are native to western North
America. Mule deer are named
after their mule-like ears, which
are about three-fourths the length
of their head.

RIGHT BOTTOM:
Great horned owl
This large owl species, *Bubo
virginianus*, is found throughout
the Americas. The two distinctive
ear-like tufts on its head that
resemble horns give the great
horned owl its name.

OPPOSITE:
Golden eagle
Aquila chrysaetos, the most
widespread species of eagle,
is found across the Northern
Hemisphere. It is also the largest
bird of prey in North America
and Mexico's national bird.

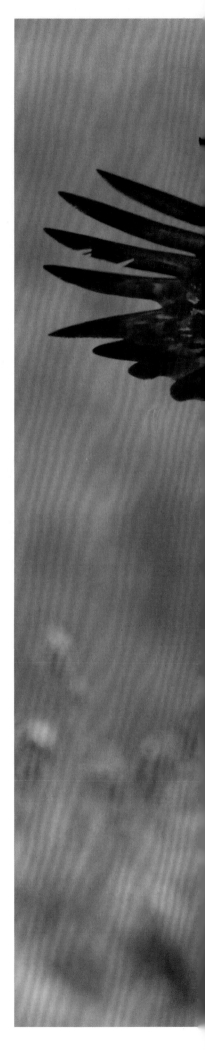

Wood bison
The subspecies *Bos bison athabascae* is the largest of the two American bison subspecies. In fact, it is the longest and heaviest land animal in North America, reaching 3.35m (11ft) in length and 1179kg (2600lb) in weight. Wood bison have a hairy coat that gets longer in the winter.

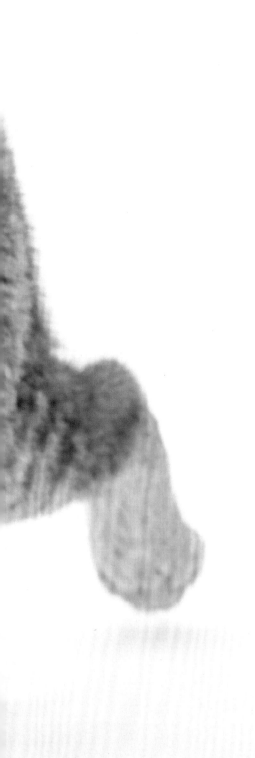

LEFT:

Canada lynx

This cat species, *Lynx canadensis*, lives in forested areas across Alaska, Canada and northern parts of the United States. Its big rounded paws covered by thick fur allow it to walk and hunt in the snow.

ABOVE:

Young lynx

A Canada lynx kitten peeks out of the den. Before birth, females prepare a den, usually inside shrubs, trees or woody debris. They give birth to between one and eight kittens.

RIGHT TOP:
Hickory horned devil
The huge, black-tipped red horns give this caterpillar its name. However, its frightening look and name are only for show – it is completely harmless. Hickory horned devils belong to the regal moth.

RIGHT BOTTOM:
Regal moth
Citheronia regalis, or the regal moth, is a common species, particularly in the American Deep South. These moths only live for about a week because, like other members of the *Saturniidae* family, they have tiny mouthparts and cannot feed.

OPPOSITE:
Snowshoe hare
This forest dweller, *Lepus americanus*, has particularly large hind feet and a winter-white coat to help it survive in the snow. In the summer, however, its fur turns brown. Its main predator is the Canada lynx.

Bobcat

Also known as the red lynx, this North American species (*Lynx rufus*) takes its name from its 'bobbed' tail. It is the smallest of the four members of the *Lynx* genus. Bobcats tend to live in warmer climates – from Canada to Mexico – so are not well-adapted to the snow.

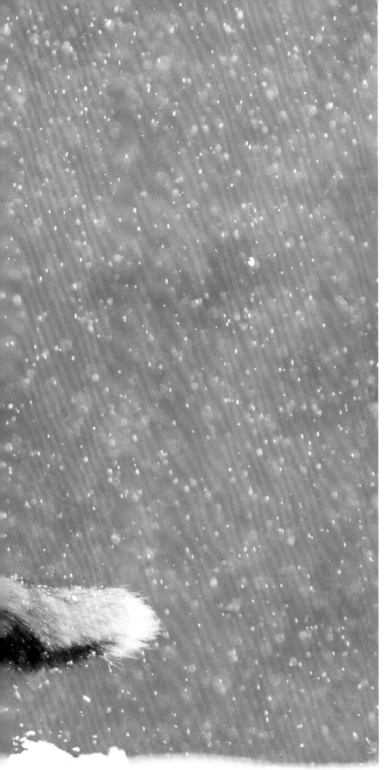

LEFT:
Red fox
The *Vulpes vulpes*, or the red fox, is one of the most widespread species. It is found in diverse habitats, including forests, throughout the entire Northern Hemisphere. Red foxes have excellent hearing, even in the snow. For example, they are able to hear a mouse squeak from 100m (328ft) away.

ABOVE TOP:
Hispaniolan solenodon
This elusive, small, shrew-like mammal is known as the Hispaniolan solenodon, agouta or *Solenodon paradoxus*. Like other solenodons, *S. paradoxus* is venomous and eats insects at night. It lives in burrows in the forests of the Caribbean island of Hispaniola.

ABOVE BOTTOM:
Common vampire bat
Named after the mythical monsters, the common vampire bat (*Desmodus rotundus*) drinks the blood of other animals as they sleep in order to survive. At night, these bats approach their prey on all fours, make a small cut with their razor-sharp teeth and lap up the blood with their tongues.

OVERLEAF:
Leafcutter ants
Named for their ability to chomp leaves, leafcutter ants are endemic to Central and South America and southern regions of the United States. They cut leaves, often many times their size, and carry them to eventually feed underground fungus farms. Leafcutter ants make up 47 species of the genera *Atta* and *Acromyrmex*.

American black bear
This bear species, *Ursus americanus*, is the most familiar and common in North America. It uses its long, curved claws to climb up trees. Despite their name, black bears can also range from blue-grey to different browns and even – more rarely – white.

LEFT:
Grizzly bear
The North American subspecies of the brown bear, known as grizzly or *Ursus arctos horribilis*, roams the forests of Wyoming, Montana, Idaho, Washington State, Alaska and Canada. Grizzlies, which are typically brown, earn their name from their fur, which can appear white-tipped or grizzled.

ABOVE BOTH:
Solitary life
Except for females and their cubs, grizzlies tend to be solitary animals. However, in coastal areas, such as in Alaska, dozens of grizzly bears gather around streams, lakes, rivers or ponds to feast on salmon during the summer spawning.

California condor
These large, imposing wings
belong to the critically endangered
California condor or *Gymnogyps
californianus* found in Arizona,
Utah, California and Mexico.
California condors are the largest
birds in North America, with
a wingspan of 3m (9.8ft).

Spider monkeys
Members of the *Ateles* genus are known as spider monkeys. This is because they look like spiders when they hang upside down from tree branches with their long, grasping tails. There are seven species of spider monkeys found in the tropical forests of Central and South America, all of which are under threat.

LEFT:

Green iguana

The dazzling green iguana, or *Iguana iguana*, is among the largest lizards in the Americas. On average, they measure about 2m (6.5ft) in length and 5kg (11lb) in weight. Green iguanas have strong jaws with razor-sharp teeth and sharp tails. Despite their name, they come in different colours.

ABOVE:

Mountain pine beetle

Native to the forests of western North America, the mountain pine beetle (*Dendroctonus ponderosae*) lives most of its life in the inner bark of pine trees. Under normal levels, its population helps the forest regenerate by killing weakened and old trees. However, in recent years, these beetles are destroying healthy forests due to warmer winters.

Wolverine
The solitary and fierce wolverine (*Gulo gulo*) is found in remote boreal forests, taiga and tundra in the northern areas of North America, Europe and Asia. Wolverines have long strong claws on their front feet to help them climb trees.

RIGHT TOP:

White-nosed coati

This tree-dwelling species, *Nasua narica*, has a long snout with a pig-like nose and a somewhat prehensile tail. Female and young male coatis live in groups called bands, which are made up of 10–30 individuals. Unlike their raccoon relatives, coatis are active during the day.

RIGHT BOTTOM:

Mantler monkey

Howler monkeys are the loudest of all monkeys which call out to alert others to stay away. This mantler howler, or *Alouatta palliata*, lives in Central and South America. The long guard hairs that cover its fur gives the howler its name 'mantler'.

OPPOSITE:

Sloth

This cute, slow-moving species is Hoffman's two-toed sloth or *Choloepus hoffmanni*, named after German naturalist Karl Hoffmann. Though related to armadillos and anteaters, it spends most of its life hanging upside down in the trees of the tropical rainforests of Central and South America.

South America

The continent of South America is filled with unique and exotic forest animals. In fact, its vast tropical rainforests – with rivers that run through them and create additional unusual freshwater habitats – make this continent one of the most biodiverse.

About 40 percent of the South American continent is covered by the Amazon rainforest. It is the largest rainforest in the world, spanning across Brazil, Bolivia, Peru, Ecuador, Colombia, Venezuela, Guyana, Suriname, and French Guiana. Within the Amazon rainforest itself, several types of forests are found – from dense, jungle-like rainforests to open forests with palms or lianas. The rainforest is home to over 3 million species: more than two million are native species of insects, including bullet ants and blue morpho butterflies. Hundreds of primate, reptile and amphibian species – from jaguars, spider monkeys, and sloths to caimans, anacondas, and poison dart frogs – live there too, as well as thousands of dazzling native birds, such as the macaws and toucans. Other South American regions, such as the Pantanal – the world's largest tropical wetland – are also full of vibrant species.

But if deforestation continues at the current rate, the forests of South America, which regulate our climate, could eventually become unable to support these healthy habitats, their unique plant and animal species, and the overall health of our planet.

OPPOSITE:
Strawberry poison frog
The poison dart frog species *Oophaga pumilio* can have 15–30 colour variations. It becomes poisonous when it eats certain subspecies of mites and ants, although it is not the most toxic poison dart frog.

ABOVE:
Harlequin poison frog
Oophaga histrionica is native
to the Chocó region of western
Colombia. Like all members
of the Dendrobatidae family –
commonly known as poison dart
frogs – O. *histrionica* is toxic.

RIGHT:
Capybara
This species, *Hydrochoerus
hydrochaeris*, is the largest rodent
in the world. Native to South
America, capybaras can be found
eating in flooded grasslands,
swimming through rivers or ponds
and sleeping along the edges of
mucky marshes.

OPPOSITE:
Keel-billed toucan
The colourful keel-billed toucan
or *Ramphastos sulfuratus* is
found in tropical forests from
Mexico to Colombia. While its
large bill appears heavy, it is in fact
a spongy, hollow bone covered in
the protein keratin. The keel-billed
toucan is a national bird of Belize.

Jaguar
The species *Panthera onca* is the
largest big cat in South America.
It has distinctive rose-shaped spots
called rosettes for camouflage.
Even those jaguars with a dark
black coat known as black
panthers have these spots.

RIGHT TOP:

Brown-throated sloth
Found in the forests of Central and South America, *Bradypus variegatus* is the most common of the four three-toed sloth species. Algae grows on the fur of these slow-moving mammals and helps them to blend in with green leaves and avoid predators.

RIGHT BOTTOM:

Silky anteater
This shy tree-dweller is a silky anteater, the smallest of all the anteaters. Silky anteaters were once considered a single species, but scientists found that they are made up of at least seven species.

OPPOSITE:

South American great horned owl
Bubo virginianus nacurutu is a subspecies of the great horned owl found only in tropical South America. Unlike the other subspecies, South American great horned owls have amber eyes rather than yellow.

LEFT:
Fleischmann's glass frog
Named after collector Carl
Fleischmann, the frog species
Hyalinobatrachium fleischmannii
is found from southern Mexico
to Ecuador. This glass frog usually
has green skin, pale yellowish
spots, yellow fingertips and a
glass-like skin covering
its stomach.

ABOVE:
Ghost glass frog
Members of the *Centrolenidae*
family are known as glass frogs.
This is because some have
transparent or translucent skin
around the belly, which helps them
stay hidden in the forest. The
family comprises two subfamilies
and 12 genera. Here, a ghost glass
frog or Limon giant glass frog
(*Sachatamia ilex*) sits on a flower.

Plumed basilisk

Known as the plumed, green or
double-crested basilisk, the species
Basiliscus plumifrons is found
from southern Mexico to northern
Colombia. To flee from predators,
it can run across water without
sinking, earning it another name:
the Jesus Christ lizard. Males have
distinctive, high crests on their
heads, backs and tails.

Hoatzin

Nicknamed the 'stink bird',
hoatzins (*Opisthocomus hoazin*)
are the only birds known to digest
food by fermentation – just like
cows or goats. Hoatzins build their
nests in branches overhanging
water in the Amazon and Orinoco
basins, and their chicks have claws
on their wings to climb back
if needed.

Six-banded armadillo

This warrior-looking species,
Euphractus sexcinctus, is known
as the six-banded or yellow
armadillo. Its armour is made
from overlapping plates of bone,
which are covered in scales of
keratin. Unlike most armadillos,
the six-banded armadillo is mostly
active during the day.

ALL PHOTOGRAPHS:
Ocelot
This beautiful wild cat species, *Leopardus pardalis*, is twice the size of an average house cat. Its spotted coat helps it blend into the forest while it hunts as well as when it sleeps on tree branches. Ocelots are found from South America all the way to the southwestern United States.

Pygmy round-eared bat
As the name suggests, pygmy round-eared bats (*Lophostoma brasiliense*) are relatively small bats with large rounded ears. They mainly feed on insects, but fruits are on the menu too.

Great potoo
This well-camouflaged animal is a species of potoo – a group of nocturnal birds of tropical Central and South America – called *Nyctibius grandis* or the great potoo.

South American tapir
Resembling a mix of a fawn and a piglet, this South American tapir calf blends perfectly into the forest. However, the white stripes and dots eventually fade, and adults are left with a dark brown coat. South American tapirs or *Tapirus terrestris* are related to horses and rhinoceroses.

Scarlet macaw
The colourful scarlet macaw, or *Ara macao*, is native to the humid evergreen forests of Central and South America. Scarlet macaws have a wide vocal range and prefer to shout rather than talk. They can also mimic human speech.

LEFT:

In flight

King vultures (*Sarcoramphus papa*) soar for hours with little effort in Central and South American skies, only infrequently flapping their wings. While in flight, their wings are held flat with slightly raised tips. King vultures can reach 67–81cm (26–32in) long with a wingspan of 1.2–2m (4–7ft).

ABOVE:

King vulture

Like other vultures, the eye-catching king vulture is a scavenger. However, the king vulture often makes the first cut into a fresh carcass with its powerful beak. Some suggest its name comes from a Mayan legend in which this vulture was a messenger between humans and the gods.

RIGHT TOP:
Bullet ant
Named for its extremely painful sting, the bullet ant (*Paraponera clavata*) lives in the humid lowland rainforests of Central and South America.

RIGHT BOTTOM:
Blue morpho
This iridescent blue butterfly, *Morpho peleides*, lives in the tropical rainforests of Central and South America. It can usually be found resting on the forest floor or low trees unless it is searching for a mate.

OPPOSITE:
Boa constrictor
The large, non-venomous species *Boa constrictor* is native to tropical South America. Also known as the common or red-tailed boa, it can grow up to 5m (16ft) long and weigh more than 45kg (100lb).

Goliath birdeater
At up to 13cm (5.1in) long and 175g (6.2oz), the goliath birdeater (*Theraphosa blondi*) is the largest spider in the world. Despite its name, goliath birdeaters rarely eat birds. Instead, their diet is made up of insects, frogs and rodents.

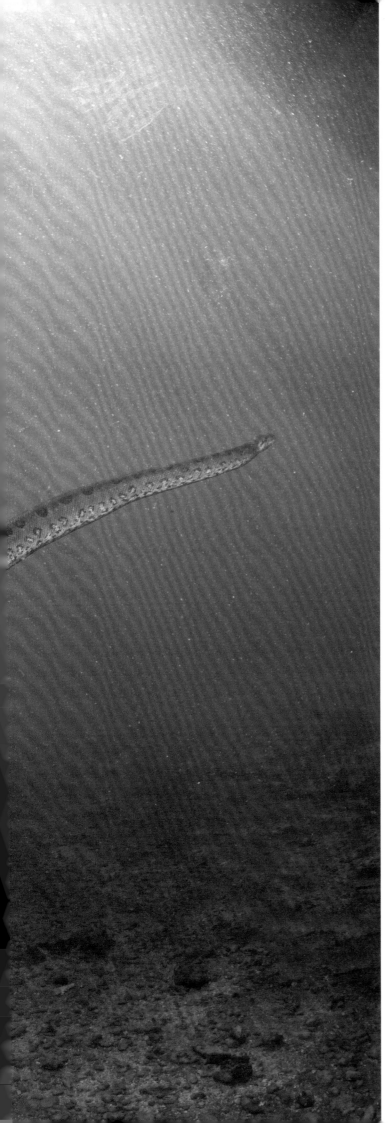

LEFT:

Green anaconda

This massive boa species, *Eunectes murinus*, is the heaviest snake in the world, weighing up to 227kg (500lb). Green anacondas spend most of their time in water and use their long, muscular bodies to constrict prey like fish, capybaras and caimans.

ABOVE:

Ambush

Green anacondas have their eyes and nasal openings on the top of their heads. This allows them to hide and wait for prey almost completely underwater before attacking.

OVERLEAF:

Squirrel monkey

Members of the *Saimiri* genus are known as squirrel monkeys. This is because they move as quickly as squirrels. Native to the tropical forests of Central and South America, squirrel monkeys are divided into two groups that are made up of five species.

Southern tamandua

Also known as the lesser anteater or the collared anteater, the southern tamandua (*Tamandua tetradactyla*) is a solitary tree-dwelling animal from South America and the Caribbean island of Trinidad. It uses its large claws to rip open insect homes and slurp up ants and termites with its long, sticky tongue.

Milkweed assassin bug
The species *Zelus longipes* is
an ambush bug that captures
prey with its sticky forelegs after
hiding. It is known to naturally
control insect pests, such as the
fall armyworm or the genista
broom moth.

Peanut bug
This odd-looking camouflaged
insect is called the peanut bug
(*Fulgora laternaria*) thanks to
its large, unshelled-peanut-shaped
head. Its head mimics that of a
lizard's to scare predators away
but is also used to knock on
trees and find mates.

Black caiman
This South American species, *Melanosuchus niger*, is the largest member of the *Alligatoridae* family. It is also one of the largest predators in the Amazon basin – the largest rainforest in the world – with most adult males measuring 2.2–4.3m (7.2–14.1ft) in length.

Europe

The smaller European continent – from the Mediterranean Sea to the Arctic Ocean – was once almost completely covered by forest. Through centuries of deforestation, over one-quarter of the continent's land remains as original forest. These include the Scandinavian boreal forests, mixed rainforests of the Caucasus, and the cork oak forests in the western Mediterranean. Most of the European forests, especially in central and western Europe, have been domesticated and are filled with crops and livestock.

In the north, the boreal forest, also known as the taiga, is composed of coniferous forests with trees like pine and fir. This is home to reindeer, moose, bear and elk. South of the taiga is a mixture of coniferous and deciduous trees, such as beech and ash, where bears, wolves, badgers, deer, foxes and squirrels, among others, can be found. Europe's hot southern edge is covered with small, drought-resistant plants and trees.

With habitat loss and hunting in Europe, many large mammals such as bears, wolves, bison, and lynxes were driven close to extinction. But these have bounced back thanks to conservation efforts in the past decades. What's more, this has helped restore the balance and health of the European forests.

OPPOSITE:
Eastern grey squirrel
Europe's grey squirrel, *Sciurus carolinensis*, is in fact native to North America. It was first introduced into England in 1876, and later into the rest of Europe in 1946.

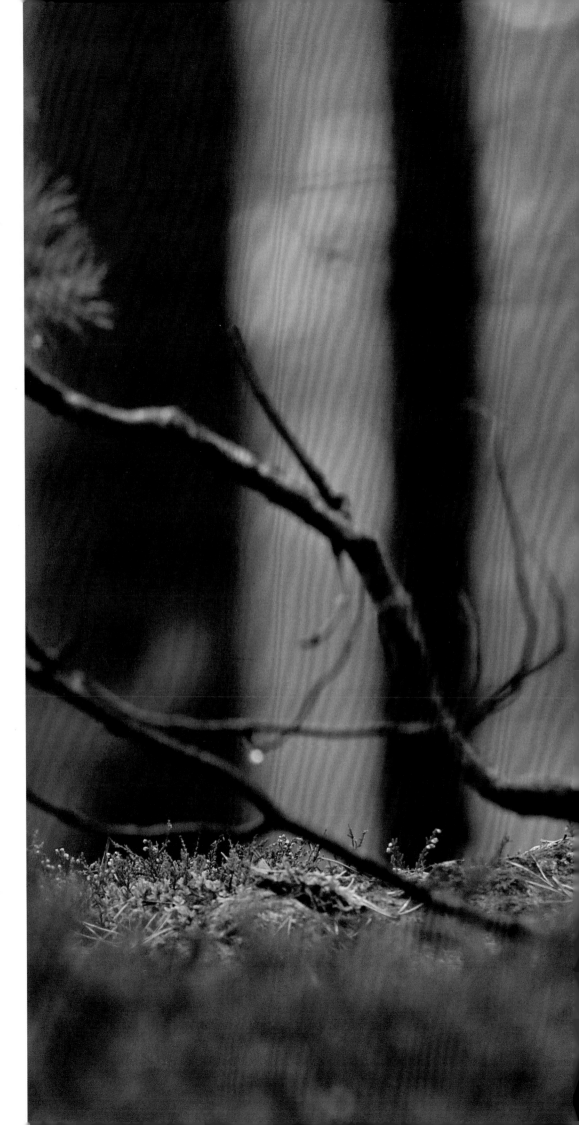

European badger
The unmistakable European badger (*Meles meles*) is noted for its black and white striped face and strong front claws, which it uses to dig for food and burrow underground homes called setts.

European pine marten
Martes martes has a distinctive
pale yellow 'bib' on its throat.
Every individual pine marten
can be identified by its uniquely
patterned bib.

RIGHT:
Beech marten
Unlike the pine marten, the
smaller beech marten (*Martes
foina*) spends more time on the
ground rather than on forest trees.

OPPOSITE:
Iberian lynx
This endangered wild cat species,
Lynx pardinus, is native to the
Iberian Peninsula in southwestern
Europe. Iberian lynxes, with
tawny and spotted coats, have a
distinctive beard, a short tail
and ear tufts.

Red deer
Standing tall and proud, red deer (*Cervus elaphus*) are social animals known for living in herds. Males, or stags, have antlers, while females, or hinds, do not. Typically, the hinds lead the herd.

RIGHT TOP:
European wildcat
This may look like a large house cat but don't be fooled – it is the European wildcat or *Felis silvestris*. However, both belong to the *Felis* genus and can interbreed.

RIGHT BOTTOM:
Eurasian lynx
As its common name suggests, the species *Lynx lynx* is found throughout most of Eurasia. *L. lynx* is the third largest predator in Europe after the brown bear and the wolf.

OPPOSITE:
Wild boar
Native only to Europe, Asia and North Africa, wild boars (*Sus scrofa*) now live on every continent except Antarctica. Wild boars live in small family groups made up of females and their young, but sometimes these groups come together and form a 'sounder'.

LEFT:

Stag beetle

Named for the massive mandibles that resemble the antlers of a stag or male deer, stag beetles are found across the world except in Antarctica. However, only males have these antler-like jaws.

ABOVE TOP:

Woodlouse hunter

As the name suggests, this spider of the *Dysderidae* family – known as woodlouse hunters – hunts woodlice and captures them by using its fangs rather than making webs.

ABOVE BOTTOM:

Large pine weevil

Hylobius abietis is a beetle known to eat the bark of seedlings and young coniferous trees like pines – sometimes also deciduous trees. This causes serious damage to the trees.

Eurasian wolf

Native to Europe and Asia, the Eurasian wolf is one of the 38 subspecies of *Canis lupus*, the grey wolf. Eurasian wolves, also known as the common wolves, were once widespread across Eurasia. But sadly, the Eurasian wolf was hunted to extinction in many countries, like the United Kingdom.

Packs

Eurasian wolves are incredibly social and live in groups called packs. Only the alpha females and males in the pack will mate, despite them consisting of about seven wolves.

Lesser purple emperor

Only the males of this alluring butterfly species, *Apatura ilia*, have iridescent blue-purple hues on their wings. Lesser purple emperors spend most of their life high in the treetops. However, males can often be spotted drinking from puddles or moist animal dung.

LEFT:

Brown bear

The impressive brown bear (*Ursus arctos*) lives in the forests and mountains of Europe, Asia and northern parts of North America. Brown bears dig dens for winter hibernation. During this winter rest, females give birth to cubs.

ABOVE:

Standing up

Like all bears, brown bears can stand on their back legs and walk a few steps. They usually do this when they are curious, hungry or alarmed.

Red fox

One of the most common carnivores, the red fox or *Vulpes vulpes* lives in Europe, Asia and North America. The fox's thick tail, or brush, helps it balance, stay warm in winter and communicate with other foxes.

Dog family

Red foxes are members of the *Canidae* family. Canids, which also includes dogs, wolves, coyotes and jackals, are social animals that live in groups on all continents except Antartica.

Solitary hunter

Unlike their dog-like relatives, red foxes have long whiskers, retractable claws and excellent night vision. They also hunt alone rather than in packs, consuming rodents, rabbits, fruit and fish.

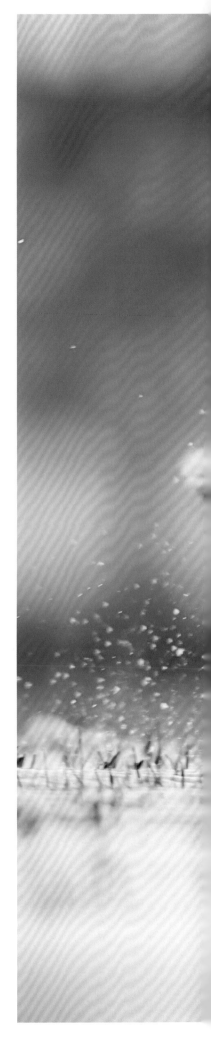

Alpine ibex
The wild goat species, *Capra ibex*, lives in the mountains of the European Alps. It is an exceptional climber thanks to its sharp-edged hooves with concave undersides that act like suction cups. In fact, *C. ibex* has been seen climbing the Cingino Dam in Italy.

RIGHT TOP:
Pool frog
This small frog species, *Pelophylax lessonae*, rarely grows more than 8cm (3in) long. Males have two large inflatable vocal sacs on the sides of their heads, which amplify their mating calls.

RIGHT BOTTOM:
Moor frog
Rana arvalis is known to spend the winter frozen and come alive after thawing in the spring. Male moor frogs are also known to turn blue during mating season.

OPPOSITE:
Fire salamander
As its name suggests, the fire salamander (*Salamandra salamandra*) has fiery orange or yellow markings on its black skin. However, it actually got its name from the old belief that it came from fire.

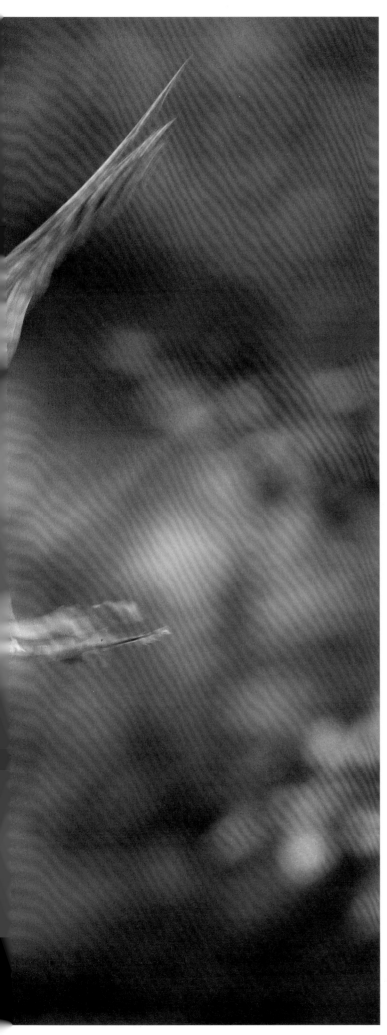

LEFT:

Eurasian goshawk

Accipiter gentilis has relatively short wings and a long tail, which make it a powerful and agile hunter of the woodlands.

ABOVE:

Eurasian treecreeper

With a curved bill and brown cryptic plumage, the Eurasian treecreeper (*Certhia familiaris*) can move slowly and carefully on tree trunks without being noticed.

Western capercaillie
Also known as the wood grouse or cock-of-the-woods, this large bird species (*Tetrao urogallus*) is found across most of Europe and northern Asia. Males are recognised by their dark grey or brown feathers and metallic green breast feathers and are almost twice the size of females.

LEFT:
Golden jackal
This wolf-like animal is the golden jackal or *Canis aureus*. However, it is smaller than its cousin the grey wolf and has shorter legs, a shorter tail and a narrower and more pointed muzzle.

ABOVE:
Wolverine
A fierce wolverine (*Gulo gulo*) stands on a tree trunk in Finland. Wolverines have long, strong claws to help them climb trees. Though they look like bears, wolverines are members of the *Mustelidae* family, which includes weasels and badgers.

Eurasian otter
This adorable river otter, *Lutra lutra*, lives near freshwater habitats across Europe, Asia and northern Africa. Using their long whiskers, river otters can locate prey in dark or cloudy waters.

LEFT:

Lesser spotted woodpecker
The species *Dryobates minor* is the smallest woodpecker in Europe, growing to 14–16.5cm (5.5–6.5in) long. The male is distinguished from the female by his bright red crown.

ABOVE TOP:

Hawfinch
This orange-hued bird with its massive bill is the hawfinch or *Coccothraustes coccothraustes*. The hawfinch's bill is powerful enough to crack open objects – even cherry stones!

Eurasian eagle-owl

Among the world's largest owls, the species *Bubo bubo* reaches 56–75cm (22–30in) in length, with a wingspan of 131–188cm (4.3–6.2ft). *B. bubo* has distinctive ear tufts and orange eyes.

Red squirrel
With a distinctive rusty red coat and ear tufts, this red squirrel (*Sciurus vulgaris*) is found in the forests of Europe and Asia. However, in the winter, its coat fades to a brownish-grey. Red squirrels have an excellent sense of smell which they use to locate nuts and seeds that they have hidden away.

Australia

Situated in the geographical region of Oceania, Australia is the smallest of the seven continents. This continent – which consists of many islands, including Australia, New Zealand, New Guinea, and the Pacific Islands – is known for its distinctive, bizarre-looking, and venomous wildlife.

In fact, the continent of Australia has the most marsupials – a group of mammals that raise their young in a pouch – and the only mammals, which can lay eggs instead of giving birth to live young, called monotremes. Marsupials, such as the tree-kangaroos, koalas, wombats, numbats, possums, and Tasmanian devils, call the forests their home. The egg-laying mammals,

the echidnas – sometimes called spiny anteaters – live in the Australian and New Guinean forests, while the platypuses are found in forests on mainland Australia, Tasmania, and Kangaroo Island.

The tropical and temperate forests in this part of the world are also home to some familiar, strange, and rare forest animals: the colourful birds of paradise, flightless birds like the emu, cassowary, kiwi, takah and k k p , well-camouflaged stick insects, tree snakes, dingoes, koalas, and flying foxes. Flying foxes, also known as fruit bats, are important pollinators and seed dispersers that mainly feed on juice from fruit but will also chew flowers for their nectar and accidentally spread the seeds.

OPPOSITE:
Goodfellow's tree-kangaroo
This long-tailed, bear-like species is the endangered Goodfellow's or ornate tree-kangaroo (*Dendrolagus goodfellowi*), which is native to the rainforests of New Guinea. Each individual has a unique pattern of brown and gold stripes on its tail.

Pink cockatoo
Cacatua leadbeateri, with its distinctive red and white crest, is known by many names: pink, Major Mitchell's or Leadbeater's cockatoo, among others. Found across Australia, pink cockatoos mate for life and raise two to three chicks together.

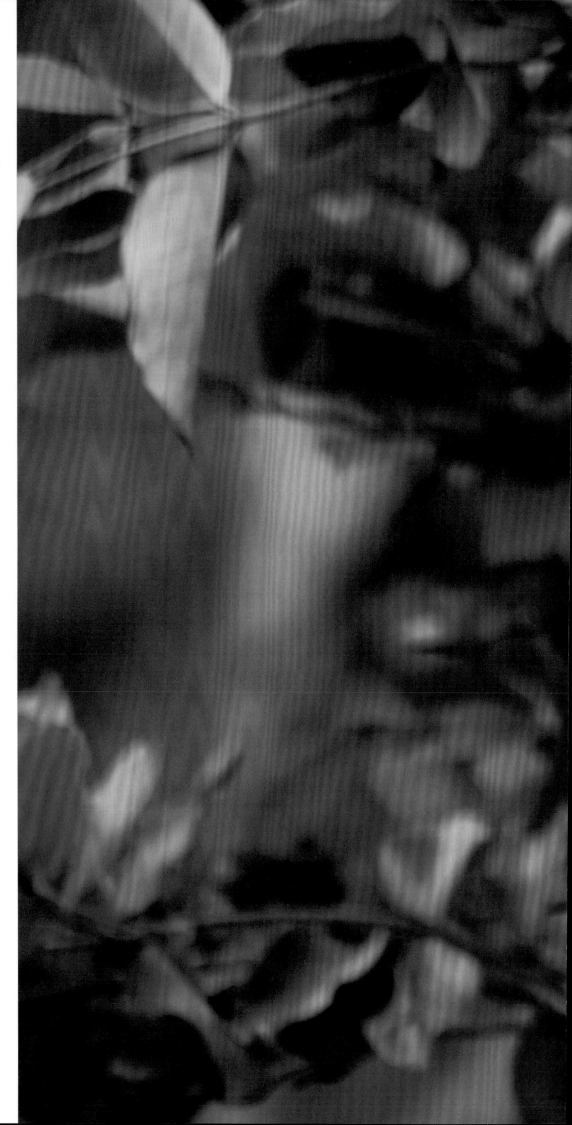

ABOVE:
Southern cassowary
This large flightless bird, *Casuarius casuarius*, lives in the forests of Indonesia, Papua New Guinea and northeastern Australia. The name 'cassowary' is derived from the two Papuan words 'kasu' and 'wari', which mean 'horned head'.

RIGHT:
Kea
Named for its loud 'kee-aaa' sounds, the kea is an endangered parrot found only on the South Island of New Zealand. Its nest is usually on the ground underneath beech trees or in rock crevices or burrows between roots that it has dug.

OPPOSITE:
Kiwi
Native to New Zealand, bird species of the *Apteryx* genus are known as kiwi. The flightless kiwi is about the size of a chicken and has tiny wings under its fluffy, hair-like feathers. It is the only bird with nostrils at the end of its long beak.

Grey-headed flying fox
With a wingspan of up to 1m (3.3ft), grey-headed flying foxes (*Pteropus poliocephalus*) are the largest bats in Australia. During the day they gather in roosting camps – which can contain tens of thousands of bats – hanging typically from trees. They leave at dusk and travel up to 50km (31mi) a night to feed on pollen, nectar and fruit.

RIGHT TOP:
Numbat

The squirrel-like numbat or *Myrmecobius fasciatus* lives in the forests of Western Australia. It nests in logs, tree hollows or burrows at night and comes out to feed on termites during the day.

RIGHT BOTTOM:
Common wombat

This cute marsupial, *Vombatus ursinus*, is noted for its cube-shaped poo! It also uses its rear end for self-defence by quickly diving into its burrow and blocking the entrance with it when threatened.

OPPOSITE:
Common brushtail possum

Like the numbat and common wombat, the common brushtail possum (*Trichosurus vulpecula*) is a marsupial or a pouched mammal. This means newborns develop inside their mother's body in a pouch.

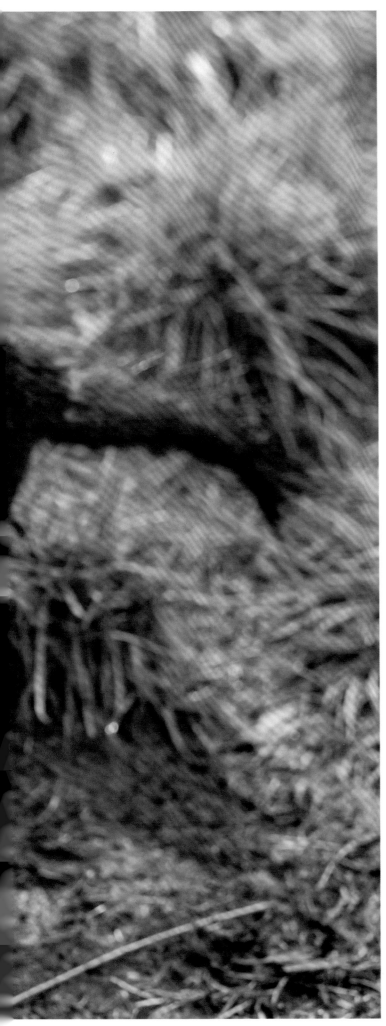

LEFT:

Tasmanian devil

At about 51–80cm (20–31in), the feisty Tasmanian devil or *Sarcophilus harrisii* is the world's largest carnivorous marsupial. When threatened, it will bare its teeth, make noises and lunge at its attacker.

ABOVE TOP:

Short-beaked echidna

This fur- and spine-covered species, *Tachyglossus aculeatus*, has a distinctive snout and a tongue specialized to quickly slurp insects from the ground. Despite being a mammal, the echidna lays eggs.

ABOVE BOTTOM:

Common spotted cuscus

At about the size of a house cat, the common spotted cuscus (*Spilocuscus maculatus*) has a distinctive curled, prehensile tail to grip onto branches, and snake-like eyes to see at night. Only the males have spots.

RIGHT TOP:

White-lipped tree frog
Nyctimystes infrafrenatus is one of the largest tree frogs in the world at 11–14cm (4.3–5.5in) in length. As its common name suggests, the white-lipped tree frog has a distinctive white strip on its lower lip that reaches up to its shoulder.

RIGHT BOTTOM:

Koala
Typically found in eucalyptus forests of southeastern and eastern Australia, the iconic Australian tree-dwelling koala (*Phascolarctos cinereus*) is a marsupial, closely related to the wombat. Newborn koalas, called joeys, develop in their mothers' pouches.

OPPOSITE:

Eastern spinebill
Found in southeastern Australia, the honeyeater species *Acanthorhynchus tenuirostris* can hover while slurping the nectar of flowers with its curved beak, resembling a hummingbird. The Eastern spinebill is on the Australian five dollar note.

LEFT:
Dingo
This wild dog or dingo is thought to be a descendant of Asian dingoes that were introduced to Australia about 3500 years ago. Dingoes can be light ginger or tan, black and tan or creamy white.

ABOVE:
Breeding
Dingoes live alone or in packs and communicate with wolf-like howls. They breed only once a year, giving birth to about five pups. But generally, only the dingoes that lead the pack are successful, as the dominant female will kill other females' pups.

RIGHT TOP:
Kākāpō
Native to New Zealand, the critically endangered kākāpō (*Strigops habroptila*) is also known as the owl parrot. In fact, it is a flightless ground-dwelling parrot that roams the forests at night. Thought to be one of the longest-living birds, the kākāpō can live for up to 100 years.

RIGHT BOTTOM:
Whiskers
The flightless kākāpō has whisker-like feathers around its beak, which help it feel its way through the forests at night.

OPPOSITE:
Lek
Males of the *Strigops habroptila* species, or kākāpō, are commonly found gathered together to engage in competitive displays and courtship rituals to attract females. This activity is known as lekking.

Blue-winged kookaburra
At about 40cm (15.7in), the blue-winged kookaburra (*Dacelo leachii*) is a large kingfisher species native to northern Australia and southern New Guinea. Blue-winged kookaburras are known for hunting snakes, which they grab and usually hit against tree branches or rocks.

Platypus

Also known as the duck-billed platypus, this unusual mammal species (*Ornithorhynchus anatinus*) looks like a mix of a duck, beaver and otter. Like the echidna, platypuses lay eggs. *O. anatinus* can be found in Australia, including Tasmania.

Bill

Platypuses have a duck-like bill which is covered with thousands of receptors that help them detect prey underwater – just like a shark does! They feed on insect larvae, worms and shrimp.

Waterproof

The platypus swims gracefully thanks to its duck-like webbed feet and beaver-like tail. Its thick otter-like fur repels water to keep it warm and dry. In addition, its eyes and ears are covered by folds of skin to prevent water from entering, whereas its nostrils are watertight underwater.

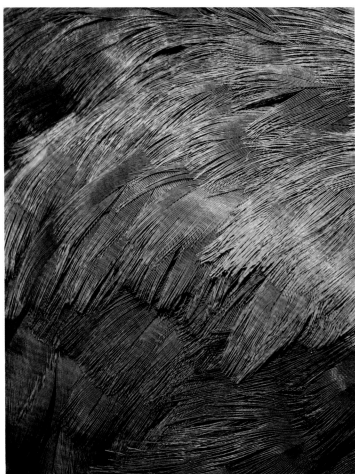

LEFT:
South Island takahē
Native to New Zealand, the South Island takahē (*Porphyrio hochstetteri*) can normally be found in alpine grasslands. However, when snow arrives, it descends to the forest or scrub. Even though the takahē is a flightless bird, it sometimes uses its tiny wings to help it move up slopes.

ABOVE:
Plumage
Both South Island takahē males and females have a silky, iridescent purple-blue plumage with a greenish back and inner wings. When startled, the bright-coloured South Island takahē will freeze in its position – but unfortunately that doesn't help it much when it is in the drab grassland!

Raggiana bird-of-paradise
This ravishing bird with long
tail feathers from New Guinea
is the Raggiana bird-of-paradise
or *Paradisaea raggiana*. Only
colourful males have this long
tail, which is used to impress the
females. *P. raggiana* is the national
bird of Papua New Guinea.

LEFT :
Splendid fairywren
The bird species *Malurus splendens*, commonly known as the splendid fairywren, is found across most of Australia. Splendid fairywrens are usually a dull colour of grey-brown. However, during the mating season, the males' plumage transforms into a beautiful bright blue colour.

ABOVE:
Courtship
Male splendid fairywrens pluck pink or purple flower petals and display them to the females as part of courtship. Like other fairywrens, they form a male-female pair, but each partner mates with other individuals as well. Despite this, the splendid fairywren will help raise all of its hatchlings.

OVERLEAF:
Victoria crowned pigeon
These charming, large, bluish pigeons with elegant lace-like crests are named after the British Monarch Queen Victoria. Native to New Guinea, Victoria crowned pigeons (*Goura victoria*) can reach up to 3.5kg (7.7lb). They also do not have a gall bladder!